Keep each layer of UTEE very hot while adding another layer. This also helps prevent blowing. A buildup of 3 to 4 layers is generally sufficient for most projects. Do not overheat, as it can burn. Overheating any embossing powder on cardstock or paper will cause it to disappear into the paper.

As soon as you remove your heat gun, the UTEE will cool. When sprinkling other embossing powders or nonmelting embellishments like Beadazzles, Diamondz, Zamora Beadz and Ultra Effects, be sure the surface is hot. If the surface has cooled, the embellishments will not adhere and when you use your heat gun, they will blow away. Exceptions to this rule are the addition of Rub 'n Buff, dry pigment powders and glitter glue, which are applied to finished and cooled projects.

When adding the last hot layer, be prepared to turn off your heat gun and quickly press inked stamp into powder. Do not wait too long or the powder will cool and an impression will be difficult to make. If you do not like the impression you made, your heat gun will erase it by melting the UTEE and you can start again.

Multiple layers of UTEE can cause paper to curl and the layers to crack. If this effect is not desired, be sure to mount your card on another sturdier card with a strong tape like Wonder tape.

UTEE can be used on many surfaces... paper, wood, glass and metal with stunning results. But remember, it is just an embossing powder and no finish is ever 100% permanent. UTEE can crack or break off after time or with wear and tear. The beauty of UTEE is you can often fix or repair those spots or make something new from something old.

Experimentation is always the key to the success of any project. So, jump right in and have fun!!

Dragonfly Card - Bronze UTEE • Clear embossing ink • Black stamp pad • 3¾" x 5" Green, 3¼" x 4½" White and 3½" x 4¾" Rust cardstock • White paper for masking • Decorative corner punch • *Repeat Impressions* dragonfly rubber stamp • Wonder Tape

Pink & Blue Frame - Clear UTEE • Clear embossing ink • Black and Blue stamp pads • 5" x 6" Blue, 4½" x 5½" Hot Pink and 4" x 5" White cardstock • 2" x 3" photo • Corner rounder punch • Triangle rubber stamp • Wonder Tape • Copper Rub 'n Buff

Twig Card - Clear UTEE • Clear embossing ink • 3" x 5" Brown and Black printed and 2½" x 4½" Natural linen mat board • Black Asian print paper • Black cardstock • 2" and 4" twigs • 24 gauge Silver wire • 6mm Red bead • Silver and Copper Rub 'n Buff

Heart Brooch - Blue and Gold UTEE • Clear embossing ink • Square, heart and small oval Stamping Shapes • 1½" hologram glitter heart • Foam mounting tape • 1" Brass cherub charm • 12mm and 6mm Gold jump rings • ½" stone heart with bail • 4 Blue 6mm flat beads • Pin back

Give your handmade cards the cool look of raindrops on glass with only one layer of UTEE. What a refreshing effect!

Tip - See Bumpy Texture technique on page 5 for these projects.

From scenic views on cards and the perfect frame for your favorite photo to a heart with a pear and an unusual clock face. Get started and try this fun 'Bumpy Texture Technique'.

Scenic Card - Clear UTEE • Clear embossing ink • Rainbow and Black stamp pads • 4¾" x 6" Lavender, 4½" x 5¾" Green and 4¼" x 5½" White cardstock • *Northwoods Rubber Stamp Co.* • Corner rounder punch • Brayer • Gold Rub 'n Buff • Wonder Tape

Gold & Copper Frame - Clear UTEE • Clear embossing ink • 4" x 5" Gold cardstock and 3¾" x 4¾" Black cardstock • 1¾" x 2½" photo • Autumn Gold Rub 'n Buff • Wonder Tape • Corner Rounder punch

Pear Card - Clear UTEE • Clear embossing ink • 4¼" x 5½" Sage folded card • 3¾" x 4¾" Black cardstock • 3½" x 4½" White paper • *Rubber Stampede* pear rubber stamp • Black ink pad • Gold paint pen •

Star Card - Clear UTEE • Clear embossing ink • Interference Green, Copper and Interference Blue pigment powder • 4¼" x 4¾" Natural linen mat board • 3⅞" x 4½" Khaki cardstock • 3½" x 4" and 3¾" x 3" pieces of White cardstock for card and star • Ellison Die Cut • 24 gauge Copper wire • 2 Orange 4mm flat beads • 2 Brass charms • 6mm Brass jump ring • Silver and Autumn Gold Rub 'n Buff • Wire cutters

Heart Trinket Box - Gold UTEE • Clear embossing ink • Small square Stamping Shape • 1¼" pear embellishment • 3" heart papier-mâché box • Metallic Green acrylic paint • Paintbrush • Mounting tape • Gold Pure Glitz Glitter Glue

1. Stamp design on paper and allow ink to dry.

Texture made with UTEE looks great!

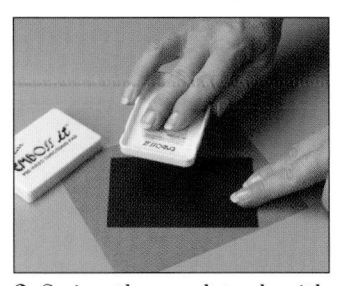

2. Swipe the cardstock with embossing pad.

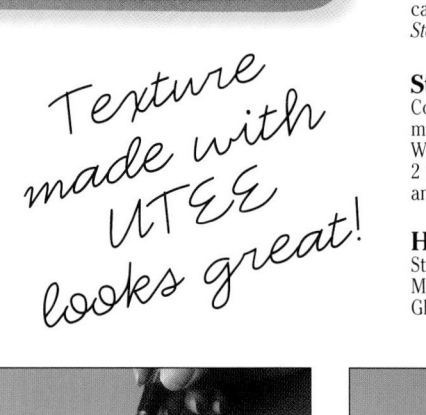

3. Sprinkle the embossing ink with UTEE.

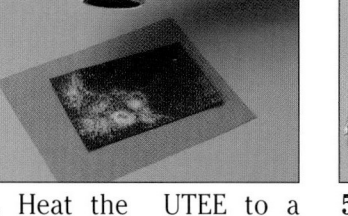

4. Heat the UTEE to a bumpy texture.

5. Apply the Rub 'n Buff or pigment powder.

Technique 1

Bumpy Texture

MATERIALS: Ultra Thick Embossing Enamel in a variety of colors • Pigment ink or Clear embossing ink • Black permanent ink • Rub 'n Buff • Wonder Tape • Foam mounting tape • Heat gun • Embossing Craft Sheet or other nonstick surface • Tiny Touch or S.O.S. Applicator

BASIC TECHNIQUE: Heating the first layer of Ultra Thick Embossing Enamel will always produce a bumpy texture that looks like raindrops on glass if it is not overheated. Overheating will make the powder go smooth.

This texture works beautifully over stamped or unstamped projects as well as all types of surfaces including CD's. If you plan to apply UTEE over a stamped card or stamped CD, it is best to swipe the project with a Clear embossing pad and apply Clear UTEE so you don't hide the design.

1. Always work on a nonstick reusable Embossing Craft Sheet.

2. If you are stamping a card, do that first and allow it to dry.

3. If you are stamping on a CD, use permanent ink and allow it to dry. Then swipe over it with Clear embossing ink, apply UTEE and heat.

4. Option: You can always change the color of the bumpy surface with the addition of Rub 'n Buff or mica powder like Pearl-Ex. When the UTEE cools, use a finger to gently rub surface with Rub 'n Buff in different colors. Apply dry pigment powder with our Tiny Touch or S.O.S. applicator.

5. Use Wonder Tape or foam mounting tape to secure layers.

Face in Blue Frame - Interference Blue UTEE • Clear embossing ink • Black stamp pad • Square Stamping Shape • Square Stamping Frame • Pearl Zamora Beadz • *Limited Edition* face stamp • Wonder Tape • Suze Gluez

Square Trinket Clock - Clear UTEE • Clear embossing ink • Black ink pad • Copper and Gold embossing powder • 4¼" wood cube box with recessed top and bottom opening • Clock fit up with hands • Assorted words and *Postmodern Design* face cube rubber stamps • Gold Rub 'n Buff • Sequins Pure Glitz Glitter Glue • Craft drill and ⅛" drill bit

CD Face Card - Clear UTEE • Clear embossing ink • Copper and Black stamp pads • 3" x 5" Rust, 2⅝" x 4½" Yellow and 2¼" x 4¼" Black cardstock • 2¾" piece of CD • *Renaissance Art Stamps* face rubber stamp • Gold Rub 'n Buff • Gold paint pen • Mounting tape • Wonder Tape

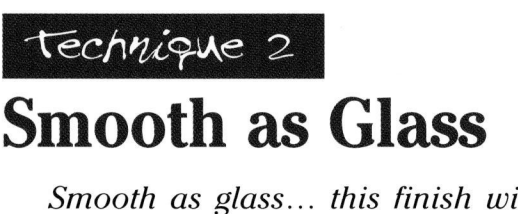

Smooth as Glass

Smooth as glass… this finish will turn your cards into works of art with the look of ceramic tiles. You'll enjoy making and giving these wonderfully unique cards!

MATERIALS: Clear Ultra Thick Embossing Enamel • Clear Embossing ink • Permanent ink and/or pigment ink • Wonder Tape • Embellishments • Embossing Craft Sheet or other nonstick surface • Card to stamp • Scissors • Additional card for mounting • Heat Gun • Diamondz • Zamora Beadz

BASIC TECHNIQUE: Two to 3 layers of heated Ultra Thick produce a smooth finish which will make a stamped card look like a tile. In order to prevent the cooled powder from cracking, it is best to mount your project on another sturdier card. Clear UTEE is not meant to be a permanent sealer. Yellowing and cracking can occur over time. If cracking occurs, and is not desired, simply reheat area gently to seal.

1. Stamp design on card using permanent or pigment ink. Allow to dry or speed process with heat gun.

2. Working on the embossing craft sheet, swipe card with Clear embossing ink, apply clear UTEE and heat.

3. Add UTEE 2-3 additional times to create tile effect.

4. All non-melting embellishments can be sprinkled in while powder is hot.

5. When completely cool, attach to a sturdy card using Wonder Tape. This tape is extremely strong and the stamped card will not lift or curl. Curling can cause the card to crack.

6. Cut other cards and use tape to add each additional layer.

Option - In lieu of swiping Clear embossing ink over your stamped card, you may apply a piece of Wonder Tape sheet over your stamped card instead. UTEE will stick to the Wonder Tape and can be heat embossed as this tape is heat resistant.

Proceed with Steps 3-5 as above.

Postage Stamp Card

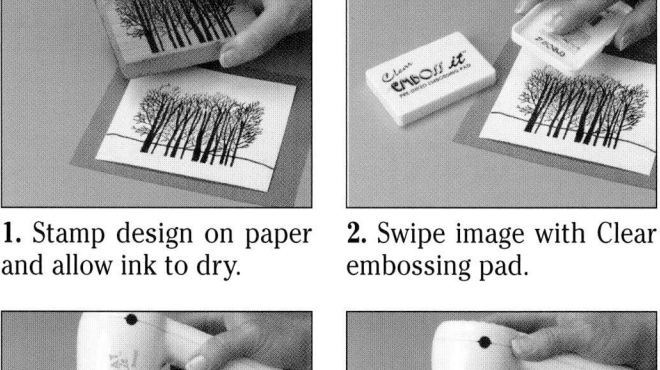

1. Stamp design on paper and allow ink to dry.

2. Swipe image with Clear embossing pad.

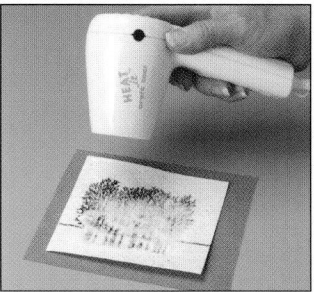

3. Apply a layer of Clear UTEE and heat.

4. Add 2 or 3 more layers of UTEE.

5. While UTEE is warm, sprinkle with Diamondz.

6. Seal with a layer of UTEE. Tape on card.

Blue Tree Card - Clear UTEE • Clear embossing ink • Black ink pad • 5" x 5½" Blue and 4½" x 5" White cardstock • Sapphire and Emerald Diamondz • *Annticipations* tree rubber stamp • Wonder Tape • Corner rounder punch

Postage Stamp Card - Clear UTEE • Clear embossing ink • 2¾" x 3⅛" and 1¾" x 2¼" cardboard • 2¾" x 3⅛" Rust and 1⅞" x 2⅜" Black cardstock • 2½" x 2⅞" Burgundy flocked paper • 2¼" x 2⅝" pastel print paper • Postage stamp • Macarena BeaDazzles • Suze Gluez • Wonder Tape

Gecko Card - Clear UTEE • Clear embossing ink • Lavender dye refill ink • Gold and Black ink pads • 5¼" x 7¼" Navy Blue, 4⅞" x 6⅞" White and 4¾" x 6¾" Tan cardstock • 4½" x 6¼" Brown corrugated paper • 5⅞" x 3¾" Gold foil paper • 4" x 5" of torn White paper • *Judi-Kins* gecko rubber stamp • Sequins Pure Glitz Glitter Glue • Jazz BeaDazzles • Suze Gluez • Wonder Tape

Bee Card - Clear UTEE • Clear embossing ink • 4" Blue and 3⅝" Cream cardstock squares • 3¼" White heavy cardstock square • 3¼" Blue print paper square • Large Brass bee charm • Gold Zamora Beadz

Leaf Card - Clear UTEE • Clear embossing ink • Black ink pad • 3⅜" x 4⅝" Hot Pink, 3" x 4¼" Cream and 2¾" x 4" White cardstock • Black and rainbow stamp pads • Red, Blue, Green and Purple ink • Tiny Touch applicators • Purple Rain BeaDazzles • Grapz Pure Glitz Glitter Glue • Wonder Tape • Ellison die cut leaf • *Stampers Anonymous* rubber stamp

Man Card - Clear UTEE • Clear embossing ink • Blue ink pad •
Blue and Fuchsia dye refill ink • 4⅞" x 5¼" White, 4½" x 4¾" Blue,
4" x 4¼" Dark Blue print and 3" x 3⅜" White cardstock • *Levenworth
Jackson* man stamp • Corner punch • Wonder Tape

Cracked Glass

MATERIALS: Clear Ultra Thick Embossing Enamel •
Card to stamp • Clear Embossing ink • Permanent ink
to stamp image • Black or colored dye refill ink •
Paper towel • Embossing Craft Sheet or other nonstick surface • Heat gun • Wonder Tape

BASIC TECHNIQUE: After heating 2 to 3 layers of
UTEE, allow to cool. Then gently bend card until cracking occurs. Rub dye refill ink into cracks with a paper
towel. This gives your project an 'aged' look. Mount
securely on another heavier card with Wonder Tape.

1. Stamp Image on card using permanent ink. Let dry.

2. Swipe over entire card using Clear embossing ink or
apply a piece of Wonder Tape over stamped card.

3. Apply Clear UTEE and heat over Embossing Craft
Sheet. Keep UTEE warm and apply another coat of
Clear UTEE. Heat again.

4. Repeat step three 2 to 3 times without adding any
additional embossing ink or Wonder Tape between
layers. After last layer, allow everything to completely cool. Sometimes putting the card in the refrigerator
for a minute will speed the cooling process along.

5. When cool, gently bend card in different directions
to form cracks.

6. Squeeze a few drops of Black or a favorite color
dye ink directly from the refill bottle on cracked surface. Wipe off immediately with paper towel. Some ink will
seep into cracks to create an aged look. Add more ink as needed or desired.

7. Secure cracked card to another, sturdier card using Wonder
Tape to prevent further cracking. The stronger the backing
card, the less likely the project will be to crack further.

1. Stamp image on paper
and let dry.

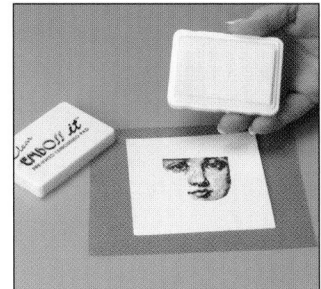

2. Swipe image with Clear
embossing pad.

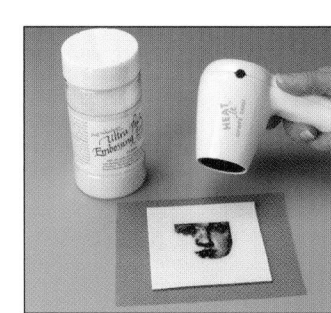

3. Apply UTEE and heat.

4. Add 2 to 3 more layers
of UTEE and keep warm as
you add them.

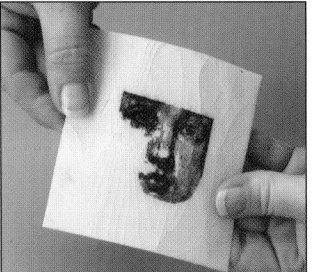

5. When cool gently bend
card to crack the UTEE.

6. Drop ink on surface and
spread with a soft cloth.

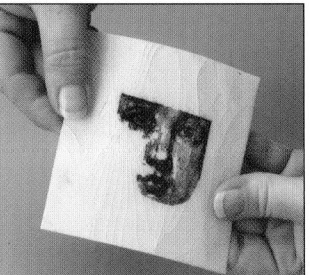

You'll love this great look!

Wall Hanging - Clear UTEE • Clear embossing ink • Black ink pad • Black dye refill ink • 4 Burgundy 4" corrugated cardboard squares • 4 Burgundy 4" flocked paper squares • 4 White 3" cardstock squares • 4 White 3" paper squares • *Postmodern Design* face cube rubber stamp • One yard of 1⅜" Burgundy velvet ribbon • Wonder Tape

Combine stamped images with cracked glass for projects that reflect the beauty of ancient times.

Terrific Tip - Use one image to make a handsome card!

Using Ultra Thick Embossing

Enamel Colors

Opulent colors, detailed stamps and glittering embellishments... These cards and brooches with a Midas touch are quick and easy to make. Begin making yours now!

MATERIALS: Ultra Thick Embossing Enamel in various colors • Colored and Metallic pigment ink pads • Black pigment ink • Heat gun • Stamping Squares • Card or mat board • Soft cloth • Wonder Tape • Pure Glitz Glitter Glue and other embellishments • Embossing Craft Sheet or other nonstick surface

BASIC TECHNIQUE: These projects use the Ultra Thick colors individually. You can use the colors as a 'backdrop' to mount things or to stamp. Apply pigment ink to your project. Apply favorite color of UTEE and heat. After building up 3 to 4 layers of UTEE, press a stamp inked with pigment ink into the hot powder.

1. Apply pigment ink to stamp and set aside until ready to use. Ink will not dry while waiting.

2. Working over the Embossing Craft Sheet, swipe pigment ink over your project. Apply first layer of colored UTEE and heat. Note: The metallic colors of UTEE as well as the Black are opaque. The colors look bright and rich when applied over Black pigment ink. The interference colors of UTEE must be applied over dark or colored ink in order to be seen. Interference color works by pigment interfering with light waves; therefore, Interference colors cannot be seen when applied over White or light colors. White UTEE should be applied over White pigment ink.

3. Keep layers of UTEE warm and apply more UTEE. Repeat 3 to 4 times without applying additional pigment ink between layers.

4. Press inked stamp into hot UTEE and release when cool, approximately 20 to 30 seconds. Note: A solid stamp will impress the color of ink. On a more open image, the underlying color of UTEE will be raised.

5. Wipe off any excess pigment ink from your project with a soft cloth.

6. Attach project to card with Wonder Tape.

7. Embellish with glitter glue, beads or wire as desired.

Egyptian Brooch - Copper UTEE • Metallic Green ink pad • 2½" x 3" Black cardstock • 2½" x 3" corrugated cardboard • *Stampland* sphinx rubber stamp • Copper glitter glue • 3 Green ⅜" x 1" curved bead spacers with 3 holes • 9 Brass 8mm jump rings • Pin back

CD Face Brooch - Gold and Interference Green UTEE • Black ink pad • Square Stamping Shape • Champagne Pure Glitz Glitter Glue • 2⅜" White cardstock square • 2½" cardboard square • 2½" Black cardstock square • Small oval Stamping Shape • 28 gauge Light and Dark Green wire • 8mm Gold jump ring • 2 Brass ½" heart charms • 1½" piece of CD • *Paula Best* face rubber stamp • Champagne Pure Glitz Glitter Glue • Pin back • Wire cutters • Wonder Tape • 1/16" circle and ¼" rectangle punches

Ruby Slipper Brooch - White UTEE • White and Green ink pads • Square Stamping Shape • *Visions of Ink* Wizard of Oz rubber stamp • Mermaid, Champagne and Ruby Slippers Pure Glitz Glitter Glue • Pin back

Bamboo Card - Platinum UTEE • Pink ink pad • 5" x 6½" White mat board • 4½" x 6⅛" Silver cardstock • 4¼" x 5⅞" Brown textured cardstock • 3¾" x 5¼" White cardboard • *Her Rubber* bamboo rubber stamp • Tiara Pure Glitz Glitter Glue • Wonder Tape

Here's more great Fun!

Asian Letters Card - Black, Copper, Gold and Platinum UTEE • Gold, Silver, Blue and Red ink pads • 5½" Black, 5¼" Plum and 5" Blue cardstock squares • 4 square Stamping Shapes • *Judi-Kins* Joy, Comfort, Peace and Hope cube rubber stamp • Gold paint pen • Wonder Tape

Heart Card - Interference Blue, Gold and White UTEE • Clear embossing ink • Metallic Green ink pad • 3⅝" x 5⅜" Red, 3¼" x 5" Plum, 3" x 4½" Grey and 2⅝" x 4⅛" heavy Lavender cardstock • 2 heart Stamping Frames • Heart Stamping Shape • Gold Zamora Beadz • Wonder Tape

1. Ink the stamping cube with pigment ink.

2. Apply the pigment ink to the project.

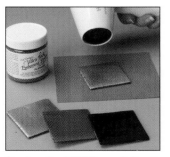

3. Apply UTEE and heat. Add 2 to 3 more layers.

4. Stamp the image in heated UTEE.

Gold Bracelet - Gold UTEE • Black ink pad • Four small oval Stamping Shapes • *All Night Media* rubber stamps • 4 Gold ¾" rune charms • 8 multi color 8mm cylinder beads • Black 24 gauge wire • Gold clasp • 6mm and 8mm Gold jump rings • Round nose pliers • Wire cutters

Clear UTEE over...
Colored Pigment Ink

Use colored pigment ink to add a rich glow to brooches, cards, frames and a trinket box. Match up your gift giving with personalities.

Fish Brooch - Clear UTEE • Silver Rub 'n Buff • Blue pigment ink • *Red Pearl* fish rubber stamp • Mermaid and Sequin Pure Glitz Glitter Glue • Blue Diamondz • 3 Blue 9mm square flat beads • Suze Gluez • 6 Silver 8mm jump rings • 3 Silver charms • Pin back

Swirl Frame - Clear UTEE • Red, Purple, Green and Fuchsia pigment inks • Gold ink pad • *All Night Media* swirl rubber stamp • 6" x 8" paper frame • Champagne and Mermaid Pure Glitz Glitter Glue

African Book - Clear UTEE • Green, Red, Lavender and Black ink pads • 2 square Stamping Shapes • 2 Moss Green 2⅜" cardstock squares • 2⅛" x 13½" Green paper strip • Autumn Gold Rub 'n Buff • Champagne Pure Glitz Glitter Glue • 24 gauge Silver wire • 38mm x 8mm wood bead • 20mm trade bead • Wonder Tape • Wire cutters

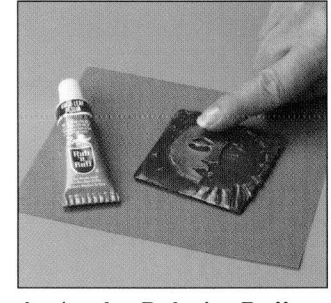

1. Sprinkle UTEE on inked stamping square.

2. Heat UTEE. Add 2 to 3 more layers.

3. Stamp image in heated UTEE. Wipe off excess ink.

4. Apply Rub 'n Buff to raised surfaces.

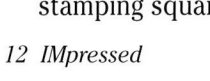

MATERIALS: Clear Ultra Thick Embossing Enamel • Colored pigment inks (Red, Purple, Blue, Green, Yellow, Pink) • Rub 'n Buff • Heat gun • Wonder Tape • Stamping Shapes • Craft frame and box • Embossing Craft Sheet or other nonstick surface • Pure Glitz Glitter Glue • Embellishments

BASIC TECHNIQUE: It is not always necessary to paint your project. You can use colored pigment inks as your base color. They may be applied to the project by patting the ink pad directly to it. This is also known as DTP (the Direct To Paper) technique. Using a direct to paper technique, apply colored pigment ink to your project. Apply Clear Ultra Thick over the colored pigment ink. If desired, stamp into project with Black or alternate color pigment ink for contrast.

1. If you wish to stamp into your design, apply Black or colored pigment ink to stamp and set it aside. The ink will remain wet until you need to use the stamp.

2. Apply colored pigment ink over your project by firmly tapping pad directly to the surface. This will give the project its color.

3. Working over the Embossing Craft Sheet, apply Clear UTEE over colored ink and heat. Keep UTEE warm.

4. Repeat step three 3 to 4 times. Note: For a more intense color, you can apply the same color pigment ink between layers of cooled UTEE.

5. On last hot layer of UTEE press inked stamp into project. Allow to cool approximately 20 to 30 seconds before pulling the stamp out.

6. Since the pigment ink often does not dry on a slick surface, wipe away ink residue by using a paper towel or soft cloth. The raised image will still be very visible.

7. As an option, apply Rub 'n Buff to highlight the raised areas of the stamped image and add glitter glue to embellish.

8. If you would like to attach project to card, use non-lifting Wonder Tape.

Sun Face Card - Clear UTEE • Purple, Red, Green and Blue pigment ink • 5½" Blue, 5¼" Gold and 5" White cardstock squares • 4 square Stamping Shapes • *Postmodern Design* sun face rubber stamp • Gold Rub 'n Buff • Wonder Tape

Trinket Box - Clear UTEE • Red and Pink pigment ink • 2" x 3" Shaker box • Small and large oval Stamping Shapes • Five ½" dice • White, Pink and Red paper • ¼" and ³⁄₁₆" hole punches • 4 Pink 3mm rhinestones • Gold, Red, Purple and Silver Zamora Beadz • Ruby Slippers Pure Glitz Glitter Glue • Wonder Tape

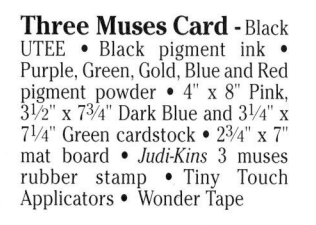

Three Muses Card - Black UTEE • Black pigment ink • Purple, Green, Gold, Blue and Red pigment powder • 4" x 8" Pink, 3½" x 7¾" Dark Blue and 3¼" x 7¼" Green cardstock • 2¾" x 7" mat board • *Judi-Kins* 3 muses rubber stamp • Tiny Touch Applicators • Wonder Tape

Gecko Card - Black UTEE • Black pigment ink • Purple, Copper and Red pigment powder • 4½" x 6" Dark Blue and 4" x 5½" Metallic Blue print cardstock • *Stampers Anonymous* rubber stamp • Gecko wood shape • Wonder Tape

Cameo Face Card - Black UTEE • Black pigment ink • Red, Gold and Green pigment powder • 3¼" x 4" Green, 3" x 3¾" Hot Pink, 2¾" x 3⅜" Dark Blue and 2¼" x 3" printed cardstock • 1⅞" x 2½" oval cardstock • *Fiddlesticks* cameo face rubber stamp • Corner rounder punch • Ruby Slippers and Mermaid Pure Glitz Glitter Glue • Mounting tape • Wonder Tape

1. Apply Clear embossing ink or Black pigment ink to stamp and set aside.

2. Rub surface of project with Black pigment ink.

3. Apply Black UTEE, heat. Add 2 to 3 more layers.

4. Stamp the heated surface with the image.

5. Apply mica pigment powder to surface using applicator. Rub n' Buff metallic creme rub may be used to highlight raised areas.

6. Make a hole and attach the beads.

Coloring the Surface with...
Mica Powders

Mica powders provide color and glitz. Add them to jewelry pieces and cards for special friends. The results are outstanding!

MATERIALS: Black Ultra Thick Embossing Enamel • Black pigment ink • Dry pigment powders in assorted colors • Tiny Touch applicators • S.O.S. applicator • Heat gun • Acrylic spray sealer • Beads and other embellishments

BASIC TECHNIQUE: Dry mica pigment powders will adhere and show up beautifully when applied over an Ultra Thick surface. Begin by inking your stamp with either Clear embossing ink or Black pigment ink. Set it aside. Apply Black pigment ink to your project. Apply Black UTEE and heat. Add 2 to 3 layers of UTEE keeping hot between layers. Press the inked stamp into the hot UTEE and release when cooled. Use an applicator to apply dry pigment powders to your Ultra Thick project. This allows you to color in very specific areas or cover an entire project. When dry pigment powders are applied over a UTEE surface, your project looks like metal. Spray seal for permanency.

Brooch with Drop - Black UTEE • Black pigment ink • Blue, Red, Purple, Green and Gold pigment powder • 3" cardboard square with torn edges • *ERA Graphics* mask face rubber stamp • Grapz Pure Glitz Glitter Glue • Pin back • 8mm Gold jump ring • Gold eye pin • Gold head pin • Turquoise 6mm bead • One 3mm and two 4mm wood beads • 2 Natural 6mm disk beads • 11mm x 15mm bone bead • Round nose pliers • Wire cutters • Craft drill and ⅛" drill bit

Necklace - Black UTEE • Black pigment ink • Copper, Gold and Bronze pigment powder • Six 1¼" cardboard squares • *Stampers Anonymous* numbers and letters rubber stamp • Eight 9mm wood beads • 2 Blue Metallic 6mm x 8mm cylinder beads • 15 Gold 10mm wood gear beads • 2 Amber 15mm x 20mm beads • 8mm wood disk bead • Beige 10mm disk bead • Black 7mm disk beads • 3mm wood bead • 8mm x 10mm Blue gear bead • Brass charm • Gold eye pin • 15 Gold 8mm jump rings • Gold clasp • 24 gauge Gold craft wire • Round-nose pliers • Wire cutters • Craft drill and ⅛" drill bit

Coloring the Surface with...

Faux Cloisonné

If you love the glowing colors of Faux Cloisonné pieces from the Orient, you will want to make all these unique projects. And best of all, they are so easy!

MATERIALS: Black Ultra Thick Embossing Enamel • Stamp with open spaces • Black and Gold pigment ink • Various colors of dry pigment powders • Tiny Touch Applicator or small cotton swab • Embossing Craft Sheet • Heat gun • Spray sealer

BASIC TECHNIQUE: This technique is one where the stamped design is pressed into hot UTEE, colored with pigment powders and heated until the raised colored design melts flat, sealing in the powders and creating the look of Faux Cloisonné.

1. Ink stamp with Gold pigment ink and set aside until needed. Ink will not dry while waiting.

2. Apply Black pigment ink to the surface of the project by pressing pad directly on surface.

3. Apply Black UTEE and heat on embossing craft sheet. Keep warm and apply more Black UTEE.

4. Repeat step three 3 times without adding any additional pigment ink between the layers.

5. On third hot layer, press inked stamp into project. Remove when cool.

6. Use Tiny Touch or S.O.S. Applicator to apply dry pigment powders to individual spaces. Note: This is a beautiful look. You may want to stop here if you prefer your piece to have a raised look. If you decide to stop here, be sure to use a glossy spray fixative on the project to seal in the dry pigment powders. Otherwise proceed to step 7 without spraying.

7. Use heat gun to reheat the powdered design. Heat until all raised areas become flat then stop. By flattening, you seal in the powdered pigments without spraying. The pattern may become slightly distorted as it flattens but remains very attractive. Note: You may stop here as you have now created a Faux Cloisonné-like design or you may continue to Step 8.

8. While Step 7 is still hot, ink a different stamp that has an open area design with a contrasting pigment ink and press into cloisonné design. Part of the project is now flat and the other part is raised. A most unusual work in progress.

Square Brooch - Black UTEE • Black and Gold pigment ink • Green, Gold, Blue, Pink, Purple and Orange pigment powder • 1" and 2⅛" cardboard squares • Tiny Touch Applicator • Suze Scoop • Tango and Jazz BeaDazzles • Suze Gluez • Foam mounting tape • Pin back

Square Earrings - Black UTEE • Black and Gold pigment ink • Green, Gold, Blue, Pink, Purple and Orange pigment powder • Two 1" cardboard squares • Tiny Touch Applicator • Tango and Jazz BeaDazzles • Suze Gluez • Suze Scoop • 2 Gold 12mm jump rings • 2 Gold ear wires • Craft drill and ⅛" bit

tip:

Melt UTEE in a Suze Scoop by holding the heat gun under the scoop filled with UTEE powder. When the powder melts, drop on the project to create little metallic balls.

Heart Brooches - Black UTEE • Black and Gold pigment ink • Green, Gold, Blue, Pink, Purple and Orange pigment powder • 2" x 3" stamping shape hearts • Tiny Touch Applicator • *Stamp Camp* peacock feather rubber stamp • Pin back

Faux Cloisonné is one of my all time favorites!

1. Cover stamping shape with Black pigment ink.

2. Apply 3 layers of UTEE, heat between layers.

3. Gently stamp image into heated UTEE.

4. Apply pigment powders in design lines.

5. Heat to flatten design.

Heart Card - Black UTEE • Black and Gold pigment ink • Green, Gold, Blue, Pink, Purple and Orange pigment powder • 4½" x 5" Black, 4¼" x 4¾" rose print, 3¾" x 4¼" Black, 3½" x 4" Lavender, 3¼" x 3¾" Gold and 3" x 3½" Turquoise cardstock • *Stamp Camp* peacock feather and *A Stamp in the Hand* Rubber Stamp • Heart Stamping Shape • Tiny Touch Applicator • Corner punch • Wonder Tape

Face Brooch - Black UTEE • Black and Gold pigment ink • Green, Gold, Blue, Pink and Purple pigment powder • 1½" mat board square • *Paula Best* face rubber stamp • Tiny Touch Applicator • Jazz BeaDazzles • Suze Gluez • Pin back

Bird Box - Black UTEE • Black and Gold pigment ink • Green, Gold, Silver, Orange, Blue, Pink and Purple pigment powder • 3" x 3½" hinged box • Tiny Touch Applicator • *Judi-Kins* bird rubber stamp

Embellishing
the UTEE surface

MATERIALS: Medium weight mat board, heavy card or Stamping Shapes • Black Ultra Thick Embossing Powder • Black pigment ink • Embossing Craft Sheet or other nonstick surface • Large stamp • Toaster oven • Heat gun • Rub 'n Buff • Diamondz • Ultra Effects • Pure Glitz Glitter Glue • Wonder Tape Sheet • Tweezers for handling hot card

BASIC TECHNIQUE: You can change the surface color and texture of your UTEE project with Rub 'n Buff and embellishments like BeaDazzles, Zamora Beadz, Diamondz and Pure Glitz Glitter Glue. This technique seems to be most effective when done with Black Ultra Thick but can be accomplished with any color of UTEE. The larger projects were melted in a toaster oven in order to keep the entire surface uniformly melted. For smaller projects, use a heat gun.

1. Ink large stamp with Black pigment ink and set aside until ready. Ink will not dry, so you have time to work.

2. Apply Black pigment ink pad directly to entire surface of project, coat with Black UTEE and heat.

3. While powder is still molten, apply another layer of Black Ultra Thick and melt. Repeat 3 to 4 times. Note: If project is unusually large, cut embossing craft sheet to fit in toaster oven or regular oven. Preheat the toaster oven and use it to melt the UTEE on your project. Always use tweezers when handling a hot project.

4. Place project on embossing craft sheet and stamp into it. Wait about 30 seconds until cool, lift stamp up.

5. When project cools, use finger to apply several different colors of Rub 'n Buff to raised surfaces. Blend different colors together for a striking look.

6. To add the dimensional embellishments, use a heat gun to reheat the selected areas while sprinkling embellishments. Be sure to keep the heat gun away from the stamped image or the image might melt. Zapping occasionally with your heat gun will seal in the embellishments. You can also use Suze Gluez to adhere embellishments. No heat is required with this method.

7. Cut Wonder Tape sheet to the size of the project and adhere to the backside. Mount another layer. Use more tape to adhere the second layer to the third layer. Repeat for additional layers.

8. Squeeze Pure Glitz Glitter Glue into the selected areas of the project for added sparkle and glitz.

African Woman Card - Black, Bronze, Interference Blue, Gold, White and Platinum UTEE • Black pigment ink • Blue, Gold and Silver pigment powder • 4" x 5½" mat board • Rainbow foil • Champagne, Mermaid and Grapz Pure Glitz Glitter Glue • Copper Zamora Beadz • Autumn Gold, Gold and Silver Rub 'n Buff • *Jenni D* African woman rubber stamp

Aztec Face Brooch - Black UTEE • Black pigment ink • 3" cardboard square with torn edges • Assorted Zamora Beadz • Suze Gluez • Sequins, Champagne and Mermaid Pure Glitz Glitter Glue • *Era Graphics* Aztec face mask rubber stamp • Autumn Gold, Silver and Gold Rub 'n Buff • Pin back

1. Cover project with Black pigment ink.

2. Apply UTEE, heat. Add 2 to 3 more layers.

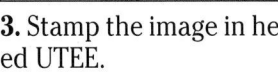
3. Stamp the image in heated UTEE.

4. Apply Rub 'n Buff to raised areas.

Give your embossed creations the glow of precious metals by simply rubbing on metallic creams. Mix colors for an even more elegant look.

Embellishing
the UTEE surface
with metallic Rub-ons

Fish Card - Black UTEE • Black pigment ink • 4¼" x 5" cardboard • Ruby Slippers and Sequins Pure Glitz Glitter Glue • Tango BeaDazzles • Suze Gluez • *Paper Parachute* fish rubber stamp • Autumn Gold, Silver and Gold Rub 'n Buff

Sun Face Card - Black, Bronze, Interference Blue, Gold and Platinum UTEE • Black pigment ink • 5½" x 6½" Green cardboard • 5¼" x 6" cardboard • *American Art Stamp* sun face rubber stamp • Macarena and Cha Cha BeaDazzles • Mixed Metals Zamora Beadz • Gold and Turquoise Ultra Effects • Mermaid and Ruby Slippers Pure Glitz Glitter Glue • Autumn Gold and Gold Rub 'n Buff • Metallic Blue and Gold 16mm disk beads • 22 gauge Gold wire • Wonder Tape • Craft drill and ⅛" drill bit • Wire cutters

Journal - Black UTEE • Black pigment ink • 4½" x 6" purchased journal • Square Stamping Shape • Jazz and Salsa BeaDazzles • Autumn Gold and Green Patina Rub 'n Buff • Suze Gluez • Champagne Pure Glitz Glitter Glue • *ERA Graphics* sun face rubber stamp

5. Apply Pure Glitz Glitter Glue to image.

6. Apply Suze Gluez to image. Add beads.

7. Press pin on back.

Terrific Earrings!

Mixing Colors
of UTEE together

You won't believe all the colorful effects that you can create by mixing UTEE colors. The possibilities are endless.

MATERIALS: Ultra Thick Embossing Enamel in all colors • Pigment inks in assorted colors • Heat gun • Wonder Tape • Assorted embellishments • Suze's Scoops • Embossing Craft Sheet

BASIC TECHNIQUE: When you sprinkle many colors of Ultra Thick together, you can create all different types of interesting patterns like mosaics, swirls or animal prints. Start with a favorite solid color UTEE on your project, keep warm and use Suze's Scoops to sprinkle in other colors of UTEE. Non-melting embellishments can be sprinkled in at any time during the heating process.

Triangle Earrings - Gold, Interference Blue and Platinum UTEE • Blue pigment ink • 2 triangle Stamping Shapes • *Red Pearl* fish rubber stamp • 2 Gold 8mm jump rings • 2 Gold ear wires • Craft drill and $^{1}/_{16}$" drill bit

Circle Card - Bronze and White UTEE • Gold pigment ink • $3^{1}/_{2}$" Gold, $3^{1}/_{4}$" White, 3" Dark Blue and $2^{3}/_{4}$" printed cardstock squares • *All Night Media* spiral rubber stamp • Wonder Tape • Foam mounting tape

Square Trinket Box - Black, White, Interference Blue, Gold, Bronze and Platinum UTEE • Gold pigment ink • $4^{1}/_{4}$" square wood box with lid • Jazz BeaDazzles • Turquoise Ultra Effects • Suze Gluez • 4 stone 16mm x 20mm beads • $1^{1}/_{2}$", 1" and $^{3}/_{4}$" buttons • Copper paint pen

Heart Frame - Bronze, Black and White UTEE • $2^{1}/_{2}$" x $3^{1}/_{4}$" Gold cardstock • Heart frame • Ruby Slippers Pure Glitz Glitter Glue • Wonder Tape

Diamond Card - Bronze, Gold and White UTEE • Black pigment ink • $3^{1}/_{2}$" x $5^{3}/_{4}$" Gold, $3^{1}/_{8}$" x $5^{3}/_{8}$" Dark Blue and $2^{1}/_{4}$" x $4^{7}/_{8}$" printed cardstock • Diamond and small oval Stamping Shapes • *All Night Media* square rubber stamp • Wonder Tape

Leaf Card - Gold and Black UTEE • Blue pigment ink • 4" x 6" Gold, $3^{3}/_{4}$" x $5^{3}/_{4}$" Black textured and $3^{1}/_{2}$" x $5^{1}/_{2}$" printed cardstock • 2 square Stamping Shapes • *Rubber Stampede* leaf rubber stamp • Wonder Tape

Can you believe this great craft? I'm just so happy to be able to share some of my favorites in this book!

1. Apply the pigment ink to the stamp.

2. Sprinkle shape with various colors of UTEE.

3. Stamp the image in the heated UTEE.

Face Charm Pin - White, Bronze and Gold UTEE • Green pigment ink • Salsa BeaDazzles • 6" shrink plastic square • *Paper Parachute* flower rubber stamp • 28 gauge Gold wire • 11mm x 14mm Gold face bead • 5 Red and 6 Green 5mm disk beads • Pin back • Wire cutters

Shrink Plastic

Bring shrink plastic to new heights of artistry. Sprinkle with UTEE and heat into glorious colors and fascinating shapes. Then use the shapes for jewelry or to embellish cards or books. Fantastic!

MATERIALS: Heat gun or toaster oven • Shrink Plastic in any color • Pigment inks in variety of colors • Heat set type of inks • Ultra Thick Embossing Enamel • Rub 'n Buff in variety of colors • Scissors • Embossing Craft Sheet or non-stick surface • Fiskars hand drill • Jewelry findings • Wonder Tape

BASIC TECHNIQUE: UTEE can be applied to shrink plastic before shrinking. No sanding is needed for this technique. Apply a heat set type of ink from the pad directly to the shrink plastic and sprinkle on the UTEE. Apply pigment ink from the pad directly to the shrink surface and sprinkle on the UTEE. Always work on the embossing craft sheet. Heat until the piece shrinks and the UTEE is fully melted. At this point you simply press a pigment inked stamp into the shrink plastic and release when cool. Remember that shrink plastic will shrink to about two-thirds of its original size, so always cut in favor of a larger size. Part of the fun and excitement of using shrink plastic with Ultra Thick is that the end result need not be a flat stamping. In fact, it is more fun to stop the shrinking process before the plastic has a chance to lay flat. This creates a very artistic effect which looks great on a card or as a book embellishment. Pieces can also be worn as jewelry. After all the shrinking and stamping is completed, you can enhance the raised areas of the surface with Rub 'n Buff. Tiny glass beads are held with Suze Gluez. You can drill into the hard shrink plastic with a hand craft drill. All jewelry findings are applied last. Wonder Tape will adhere shrink plastic to a card surface.

Dragonfly Brooch - Gold and Bronze UTEE • Green pigment ink • 12" x 6" shrink plastic • *Stampers Anonymous* rubber stamp • Tango and Macarena BeaDazzles • 2 Copper 5mm x 11mm beads • Black 7mm x 9mm bead • 2" x 1½" Copper dragonfly charm • 28 gauge Copper wire • Pin back • Craft drill and ⅛" drill bit • Wire cutters

Card with Charm - Clear, Bronze and Gold UTEE • Green pigment ink • Pink, Yellow, Purple, Red and Turquoise dye refill ink • 9" x 6" shrink plastic • 4¼" x 5¼" Yellow, 4" x 5" Rust, 3¾" x 4¾" printed and 3" x 3¾" White cardstock • *Judi-Kins* word rubber stamp • 28 gauge Gold wire • Brass charm • Craft drill and ⅛" drill bit • Wire cutters

Star Earring Pattern Cut 2

Heart Card Pattern Cut 5

1. Cut out shapes from shrink plastic.

2. Apply heat bonding ink to the plastic.

3. Sprinkle the ink with colored UTEE.

4. Shrink plastic with heat gun or toaster oven. While warm, stamp image.

5. Drill hole in project.

Asian Book - Black UTEE • Gold and Black pigment ink • Gold Wonder Beads • Ruby Slippers Pure Glitz Glitter Glue • Suze Gluez • 5" shrink plastic square • *Raindrops on Roses* Asian characters and *Her Rubber* coins rubber stamps • 3" x 5" purchased book with ribbon closure • Red and Metallic Gold markers • Wonder Tape

Star Earrings - Interference Green UTEE • Green pigment ink • Two 5" shrink plastic squares • *Paper Parachute* flower rubber stamp • Silver Rub 'n Buff • 2 Gold 8mm jump rings • 2 Gold ear wires • Craft drill and ⅛" drill bit

Hearts Card - Bronze and Gold UTEE • Blue and Black pigment ink • Five 3" x 6" shrink plastic squares • 3½" x 8½" mat board • 3½" x 8½" metallic print, 3⅛"x 7⅞" Blue and 2½" x 8" print cardstock • 4 Gold 6mm and 8 Gold 8mm jump rings • 4 Blue 4mm disk beads • Wonder Tape • 2 Gold 4mm brads • Craft drill and ⅛" drill bit

UTEE Stamping

into UTEE using regular embossing powder

For beautiful textures, press a rubber stamp dipped in embossing powder into your UTEE projects. Combine contrasting colors for stunning effects.

MATERIALS: Ultra Thick Embossing Enamel • Regular fine or textured embossing powders • Pigment ink • Embossing Craft Sheet • Heat gun • Small detail brush • Fiskars hand drill • A rubber stamp with good texture or an easily defined image • Embellishments

BASIC TECHNIQUE: Ink stamp with pigment ink. Pour a small amount of a Verdigris or other regular embossing powder onto the Embossing Craft Sheet. Tap inked stamp into powder to coat the stamp. Use a fine detail brush to eliminate powder in unwanted areas of the stamp. Press the stamp into the heated project and remove when cool. The heat will bond the 2 embossing powders. The design or pattern will show up as a texture.

3 Diamonds Card - Interference Blue, Gold and Interference Green UTEE • Pink, Chinese Red and Cobalt Blue embossing powder • 5" x 8¼" Tan, 4½" x 7¾" Black border print and 3¼" x 6¼" Beige cardstock • 3 diamond Stamping Shapes • *American Art Stamp* heart rubber stamp • Wonder Tape

Horse Card - Bronze and Gold UTEE • Verdigris embossing powder • 4½" x 5½" Gold, 4¼" x 5¼" Green and 4" x 5" Dark Blue cardstock • 3" x 4" mat board • Square Stamping Shape • Suze Gluez • *Magenta* horse and *A Stamp in the Hand* words rubber stamps • Sapphire Diamondz • ¼" rectangle punch • Wonder Tape

Horse Brooch - Bronze UTEE • Verdigris embossing powder • Square Stamping Shape • *Magenta* horse rubber stamp • Multi color Zamora Beadz • Suze Gluez • Copper glitter glue • Pin back

Using this technique you can create a variety of images in different styles. You'll love how easy it is and you'll love the compliments too!

1. Accent edges of project with hole punch.

2. Sprinkle regular embossing powder on Craft Sheet.

3. Tap the stamp into the powder lightly.

4. Press the image into the heated UTEE.

Geisha Card - White UTEE • Bronze embossing powder • 3" x 5" Dark Blue, 3½" x 4" Silver, 3" x 3¼" Dark Blue, 2½" x 3" White, 2¼" x 2¾" Dark Blue and 1⅞" x 2⅝" Burgundy cardstock • Square Stamping Shape • ⅛" diamond punch • *Art Accents* geisha rubber stamp • Pearl and Red Zamora Beadz • Suze Gluez • Ruby Slippers Pure Glitz Glitter Glue • 1¼" Silver Asian character charm • 8mm Silver jump ring • Wonder Tape • Craft drill with ⅛" drill bit

Geisha Blue Brooch - Interference Blue UTEE • Gold embossing powder • Square Stamping Shape • *Art Accents* geisha rubber stamp • Pearl Zamora Beadz • Suze Gluez • Pin back

Red Brooch - White UTEE • Bronze embossing powder • Square Stamping Shape • ⅛" diamond punch *Art Accents* geisha rubber stamp • Pearl and Red Zamora Beadz • Suze Gluez • Ruby Slippers Pure Glitz • 1¼" Silver Asian character charm • 8mm Silver jump ring • Wonder Tape • Craft drill with ⅛" drill bit

1. Apply pigment ink to wood shape.

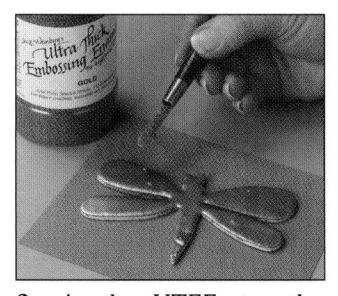

2. Apply UTEE to the shape, heat. Add one to two more layers.

3. Sprinkle a second color of UTEE on wings and heat.

4. Add glue and sprinkle with BeaDazzles.

5. Apply the rhinestones with tweezers.

Cat Card - Black UTEE • 4½" x 5¾" Metallic Green, 4¼" x 5½" Metallic Copper and 4" x 5¼" Metallic print cardstock • 4" wood cat shape • Disco Ball BeaDazzles • Suze Gluez • Two 4mm rhinestones • Wonder Tape

Ghost Card - White and Black UTEE • 4¾" x 6" Black, 4¼" x 5½" Orange and 4" x 5" Black Metallic print cardstock • 4" wood ghost shape • Disco Ball BeaDazzles • Two 4mm rhinestones • Suze Scoop • Wonder Tape

Bird Card - Bronze, White and Gold UTEE • Purple, Green rainbow and Fuchsia ink pads • 5" x 6½" Dark Blue, 4¾" x 6" Lavender and 4¼" x 5¾" Raindrop print cardstock • 5¾" wood bird shape • *Posh Impressions* flower stamp • Disco Ball BeaDazzles • Suze Gluez • 4mm rhinestone • Wonder Tape • Foam mounting tape • Gold paint pen

Embellishing Wood Pieces
Craft Shapes

Apply UTEE to wood shapes, heat and attach to a card for raised designs that are brightly colored and richly textured.

MATERIALS: Unfinished wood craft shapes • Ultra Thick Embossing Enamel in all colors • Black pigment ink • White pigment ink • Metallic paint markers • Ultra Effects • Diamondz • Suze Gluez • Suze's Scoops • Rhinestones • Tweezers • Embossing Craft Sheet • Foam mounting tape • Wonder Tape

BASIC TECHNIQUE: Wood craft shapes can be transformed into dimensional pieces of art. No need to prepare the wood surface. Simply apply pigment ink to the wood shape, sprinkle on UTEE and heat.

1. Apply pigment ink to craft shapes and coat with Ultra Thick Embossing Enamel. All shapes use Black pigment ink as the undercoating except the ghost which used White pigment ink.

2. Heat shape over Embossing Craft Sheet until UTEE is melted. Keep hot as you add layers of UTEE.

3. Using Suze's Scoops, mix and match UTEE colors by sprinkling one color over another.

4. Sprinkle nonmelting embellishments into UTEE while hot.

5. When project is cooled, use Suze Gluez to adhere BeaDazzles, Zamora Beadz or other embellishments.

6. Melt UTEE in a Suze Scoop and drizzle over project to make eyes.

7. Use tweezers to assist in setting rhinestones into hot UTEE. Hot UTEE acts like a glue.

8. If desired, use metallic markers to paint around the unfinished edges.

Giraffe Card - Bronze and Black UTEE • Black ink pad • 4½" x 5¾" Black, 4¼" x 5½" Blue, 4" x 5¼" Metallic print and 3¾" x 5" Metallic Rainbow print cardstock • *Ink Blocks* African rubber stamp • 3½" wood giraffe shape • 4mm rhinestone • Wonder Tape • Foam mounting tape • Gold paint pen

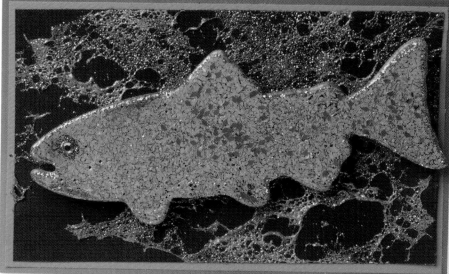

Dragonfly - Interference Blue and Gold UTEE • Black ink pad • 4⅝" x 5¾" Plum and 4⅜" x 5 ½" Turquoise cardstock • 4" x 5" rose print paper • Jazz BeaDazzles • Suze Gluez • 4½" wood dragonfly shape • Six 4mm rhinestones • Wonder Tape • Foam mounting tape

Fish Card - Interference Green and Black UTEE • Clear embossing ink • Gold and Bronze embossing powder • 3½" x 5¾" Metallic Copper, 3¼" x 5½" Turquoise and 3" x 5¼" Black cardstock • Mermaid and Champagne Pure Glitz Glitter Glue • Sapphire Diamondz • Gold Ultra Effects • 5½" wood fish shape • 4mm rhinestone • Wonder Tape • Foam mounting tape • Gold paint pen

Star Placecard - Gold and Clear UTEE • Clear embossing ink pad Turquoise and Gold pigment powder • 2½" x 5¼" Gold folded and 2" x 5" Dark Blue cardstock • White cardstock to back stars • *All Night Media* swirl and *Inkadinkadoo* dream rubber stamps • White shelf liner • Champagne Pure Glitz Glitter Glue • Wonder Tape

Placecard Star Pattern

Hearts Card - Gold and Bronze UTEE • Metallic Copper pigment ink • 4½" x 5¾" Dark Blue, 4¼" x 5½" Rust and 3¾" x 5" Green rainbow print cardstock • 2" x 4" Metallic Blue rainbow paper • Ellison 2" x 4" die cut heart • *Mail Expressions* pinwheel rubber stamp • White shelf liner • Turquoise Ultra Effects • Wonder Tape

Placecard Star Pattern

Butterfly Card - Gold, Interference Blue and Bronze UTEE • 4¾" x 5¾" Plum, 4¼" x 5½" Dark Blue and 4" x 5" Metallic print cardstock • Ellison 5" x 3½" butterfly die cut • White shelf liner • Amethyst Diamondz • Suze Gluez • Jazz and Waltz BeaDazzles • Wonder Tape • Corner punch

Stamping into...
Rubber Shelf Liners

The simple shelf liner becomes a gorgeous work of art with the addition of UTEE and sparkling glitter. Unbelievable!

MATERIALS: Heavy duty rubber shelf liner • Ultra Thick Embossing Enamel in all colors • Metallic pigment ink • Non-melting embellishments • Wonder Tape • Heat gun • Stamp with either a strong solid image or a very good open image

BASIC TECHNIQUE: The thicker rubber shelf liner provides a soft, flexible but nicely textured surface for stamping. It comes in a variety of colors. If you wish to have the original color remain, use both clear embossing ink and clear UTEE on the surface. If you'd like to change to the color of the shelf liner, use either a colored pigment ink or colored UTEE on the surface.

1. Cut shelf liner to desired size or shape.
2. Ink stamp with metallic pigment ink.
3. Apply a very light coat of pigment ink to surface of shelf liner.
4. Sprinkle just one layer of UTEE on surface and heat.
5. If you wish to add any non-melting embellishments, sprinkle them in while you are heating the surface.
6. If you wish to add other colors of UTEE to shelf liner, sprinkle in while heating. The shelf liner may shrink a bit while heating and may even produce a little bit of a fume.
7. Press inked stamp into liner and release when cool.
8. Attach shelf liner using Wonder Tape.

1. Cut rubber shapes and apply pigment ink.

2. Sprinkle with UTEE and heat.

3. Sprinkle with non-melting embellishments while still warm.

4. Reheat surface and stamp image.

Purse Necklace by Malana Watt-Corn

Purse Necklace - Bronze UTEE • Verdigris pigment ink • *Stamp Zia* ginko leaves rubber stamp • Premade 4½" x 4¾" Black leather pouch • Black shelf liner • 3½" Copper crafter's mesh square • Gold Wonder Beads • Two 18" for lacing, three 9" for fringe and 18" for handle pieces of Black 2mm leather cord • 15 assorted 8mm to 10mm beads • 20 and 28 gauge Copper and 28 gauge Black wire • Round-nose pliers • Wire cutters • ⅛" punch

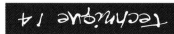

Marbled Watercolor Effect

Watercolor crayons marbled on an embossed background give your paper art pieces a finish that you will just love!

MATERIALS: White, Platinum, Bronze or Gold Ultra Thick Embossing • Water color crayons • Hair pick or other thin graining tool • Heat gun • Rubber stamp • Pigment ink • Wonder Tape • Embellishments

BASIC TECHNIQUE:

1. Apply pigment ink to project.
2. Apply UTEE in your color of choice to surface of project and heat. Repeat 2 to 3 times building up layers
3. Allow the last layer to cool slightly but not become cold.
4. Using watercolor crayons, draw lines on project in multi color stripes until the entire surface is covered. The warmth from the semi-cooled UTEE will help the watercolor crayons melt.
5. Using heat gun, warm the colored surface and use hair pick to pull the colors up as you would when marbling. Colors should be pulled in the opposite direction from the way they were colored. The combination of crayon color choices and base color of UTEE will determine how the final marbling colors appear.
6. Press inked stamp into warm surface and release when cool.
7. Mount the project on a card with Wonder Tape. Embellish with glass beads using Suze Gluez. Earrings, pin back and hanging charms are all added after marbling is completed and has cooled.

Leaf Card - Watercolor crayons • Hair pick • 4¼" x 4¾" Rust folded card • 3½" x 4⅝" Green, 3¼" x 4⅝" Tan, 2⅞" x 4⅛" Dark Blue and 2½" x 3¾" White printed cardstock • Ellison 2" x 3½" leaf die cut • Gold Wonder Effects • Suze Gluez • 18" pieces of assorted fibers • Two Natural 8mm x 38mm wood beads • Wonder Tape

Half Heart Earrings - Gold UTEE • Watercolor crayons • *American Art Stamp* Rubber Stamp Co. • Heart Stamping Shape • Suze Scoop • 2 Gold 8mm Gold jump rings • 2 Gold ear wires • Craft drill and ⅛" drill bit

1. Cover the shape with pigment ink.

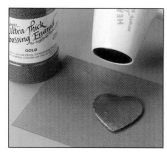

2. Apply 2 layers of UTEE, heating between layers.

3. Color stripes with watercolor crayons.

4. Heat and make design with hair pick.

5. Cut shape in half and punch holes. Add the earring findings.

Thunderbird Card - Gold UTEE • Watercolor crayons • 5" x 5⅝" Green, 4¾" x 5½" Dark Blue and 4½" x 5¼" White rainbow print cardstock • 4½" x 4" thunderbird wood shape • Hair pick • 28 gauge Gold wire • 9mm cylinder beads • Two 9mm Blue bead dangle • Gold and Black paint pens • Gold 8mm jump ring • Brass boot charm • Wonder Tape • Wire cutters

Square Card - White UTEE • Watercolor crayons • 4⅛" x 4½" Dark Blue, 3¾" x 4" Green 3½" Natural square with torn edges and 2½" x 2¾" Metallic print cardstock • Square Stamping Shape • *A Stamp In The Hand* rubber stamp • Hair pick • Gold paint pen • Gold Wonder Beads • Suze Gluez • Wonder Tape

Using Foils
with UTEE

For pure glitz, all you need is metallic foil pressed into your warm UTEE. Cards reflect every color of the rainbow.

MATERIALS: Colored and Clear Ultra Thick Embossing Enamel • Metallic foil sheets • Clear embossing pad • Pigment ink • Heat gun • Rubber stamp • Embellishments • Wonder Tape

BASIC TECHNIQUE: Hot Ultra Thick often acts as a glue. In this technique, brightly colored foil will adhere to the hot UTEE.

1. Apply pigment ink to stamp and set aside

Square Frame Card - Black and Clear UTEE • Clear embossing ink • Black pigment ink • Metallic foil • Square Stamping Frame • 4" Blue, 3¾" Green and 3¼" Black print cardstock squares • *Stamp Cabana* texture rubber stamp • Wonder Tape

Geisha Card - Black and Clear UTEE • Clear embossing ink • Verdigris pigment ink • Metallic foil • Square Stamping Shape • 4" x 5" Plum, 3¾" x 4¾" Blue, and 3¼" x 4¼" White print cardstock • *Art Accents* geisha rubber stamp • Gold Wonder Beads • Suze Gluez • Wonder Tape

Warrior Card - Black and Clear UTEE • Clear embossing ink • Purple pigment ink • Metallic foil • 4¼" x 5½" Plum and 4" x 5¼" Dark Blue cardstock • 3¼" x 4½" mat board • *Stamp Francisco* African warrior rubber stamp • Copper Zamora Beadz • Gold Wonder Beads • Suze Gluez • Ruby Slippers Pure Glitz Glitter Glue • Wonder Tape

1. Cut Wonder Tape Sheet into a variety of unusual shapes and place on card.

2. Press foil on tape and pull off.

2. Apply pigment ink to project and apply UTEE in chosen color. Repeat 2 additional times for a total of 3 applications of UTEE.

3. On this last hot layer of UTEE, place colored foil on hot surface with the color side of the foil facing up. Do not touch this surface. It will remain hot for a while.

4. Remove foil when cool. A lovely layer of foil will remain.

5. Apply a thin layer of Clear embossing ink directly from the pad on the foiled surface

6. Apply Clear UTEE to the surface and heat. This will produce a beautiful finish on the foil.

7. On occasion while heating this surface, the foil may separate and holes will form. There is no way to close the holes. Sprinkle UTEE into those spaces while warm to fill spaces with color.

8. Press an inked stamp into heated surface. Release when cool.

9. Add embellishments as an option using Suze Gluez and assorted glass beads.

10. Optional: Foils will also stick to Wonder Tape. Use this tape to create a pattern on which to place the foil. Proceed to Step 6.

Lady Frame Card - Black and Clear UTEE • Clear embossing ink • Red pigment ink • Metallic foil • Stamping frame • 4½" x 5½" Blue, 4½" x 5⅛" Plum, 4" x 5" Blue and 3¾" x 4½" White cardstock • *Renaissance Art Stamps* face rubber stamp • Wonder Tape

Cow Head Card - Black and Clear UTEE • Clear embossing ink • White and Verdigris pigment ink • Metallic foil • Square Stamping Frame • 4½" x 4¾" Turquoise folded card • 4¼" x 4½" Black stripe cardstock • 4½" Yellow and 4½" Rainbow print cardstock squares • 4" wood cow head • *Uptown Design* leaf and *A Stamp in the Hand* words rubber stamps • Wonder Tape

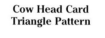

Cow Head Card Triangle Pattern

Cow Head Card Triangle Pattern

3. Apply one layer of UTEE. Heat to a bumpy texture.

4. Apply UTEE to frame and heat. Add one to two more layers.

5. Press foil on warm UTEE, cool and pull off.

6. Stamp image, cut out and glue in frame.

Magic Carpet Card - Technique 8. Black and Clear UTEE • Black and Verdigris pigment ink • 4¾" x 6⅞" and two 3" x 4½" pieces White cardstock • 4" x 6½" mat board • *Paper Parachute* rubber stamp • Gold Rub 'n Buff • Gold Wonder Beads • Mermaid Pure Glitz Glitter Glue • Suze Gluez • Wonder Tape • Foam mounting tape

Octagon Box - Technique 6. Black UTEE • Black pigment ink • Assorted colors of pigment powder • 4" octagonal papier mâché box • *Stampers Anonymous* letter rubber stamps • 3 soft drink can tabs • Copper and multi color Zamora Beadz • Gold Wonder Beads • Champagne Pure Glitz Glitter Glue • Suze Gluez • Copper glitter glue • ¾" Brown button • 10mm Red bead • Brass charm • Gold 8mm jump ring • 28 gauge Gold wire • Wire cutters • Craft drill and ⅛" drill bit

Blue & Gold Card - Technique 14. Platinum UTEE • Gold embossing powder • Verdigris pigment ink • Watercolor crayons • 4½" x 5¼" Dark Blue folded card • 4" x 4½" Natural paper with torn edge • 3" Dark Blue, 2½" Beige and 2¼" Black Metallic print cardstock squares • Square Stamping Shape • Hair pick • *Paula Best* Rubber Stamp • Gold Rub 'n Buff • Gold Wonder Beads • Suze Gluez • Wonder Tape

Green Box - Technique 11. Platinum UTEE • Black pigment ink • Verdigris embossing powder • *The Rubbernecker* rubber stamp • Hematite and Green 6mm beads • 22mm x 29mm bone bead • 28 gauge Silver wire • Craft drill and ⅛" drill bit • Wire cutters